The Three I's: Imitation, Inspiration and Innovation

By

Mohsin Gulzar

NOTION PRESS

India. Singapore. Malaysia.

Published by Notion Press 2021
Copyright© **Mohsin Guizar** 2021
All Rights Reserved.

ISBN: 9798885308120

This hook has been published with all reasonable efforts taken to make the material error-free after the consent of the author. No part of this hook shall he used, reproduced in any manner whatsoever without written permission from the author, except in the case of brief quotations embodied in critical articles and reviews.

The Author of this hook is solely responsible and liable for its content including hut not limited to the views, representations, descriptions, statements, information, opinions and references ["Content"]. The Content of this hook shall not constitute or he construed or deemed to reflect the opinion or expression of the Publisher or Editor. Neither the Publisher nor Editor endorse or approve the Content of this hook or guarantee the reliability, accuracy or completeness of the Content published herein and do not make any representations or warranties of any kind, express or implied, including hut not limited to the implied warranties of merchantability, fitness for a particular purpose. The Publisher and Editor shall not he liable whatsoever for any errors, omissions, whether such errors or omissions result from negligence, accident, or any other cause or claims for loss or damages of any kind, including without limitation, indirect or consequential loss or damage arising out of use, inability to use, or about the reliability, accuracy or sufficiency of the information contained in this hook.

Imitation distorts originality and over-imitation suffocates the God-given creativity and innovativeness within. Let's get inspired from others and imitate in an innovative way i.e., to create a new thing out of something.

— Mohsin Gulzar

CONTENTS

Introduction

Imitation is not a bad thing if done innovatively. Constantly imitating others will always harm us because it means we are not using our God-given ability inside and it will always cause us to lose sight of our own identity.

In this book, I discuss the significance of inspiration over imitation as well as how it is critical in the formation and development of an innovative idea in a person's mind. It changes a person's perception of their own abilities and catapults them from apathy to possibility. Inspiration motivates people to work hard and achieve their goals, which leads to success.

Innovation refers to something new or to a change made to an existing product, idea, or field. New ideas come from the flashes of inspiration when people are in a relaxed or inspiring situation. So, inspiration has a very important role in making an innovation.

1. The First 'I': Imitation

Imitation is derived from an Old French word *imitacoin* which means "emulation; act of copying." It is also derived from Latin word *imitationem* (nominative imitatio) which means "a copying, imitation." Imitation is defined as the act of copying, or a fake or copy of something. Imitation is an advanced behavior whereby an individual observes and replicates another's behavior. Imitation is also a form of social learning that leads to the "development of traditions, and ultimately our culture. It allows for the transfer of information (behaviours, customs, etc.) between individuals and down generations without the need for genetic inheritance."

George Romanes (1884) defined imitation as the optical discernment and replication of an action and it accommodates functions that are crucial for gregarious interaction (Heyes, 2018; Whiten & Ham, 1992). For instance, imitating another person's action (either simultaneously or with a temporal delay) was proposed to act as a gregarious glue that fosters interpersonal affiliation. Support for this notion emanates from studies exhibiting that imitation increases sympathy and prosocial demeanor (e.g., Catmur and Heyes, 2013; Chartrand and Bargh, 1999; van Baaren, Holland, Steenaert, and van Knippenberg, 2003). This research most typically analyzed the imitation of perceived forms of kineticism of another person (i.e., how an action was performed by this person). In integration to such perceptions, the action could be additionally perceived in terms of the goal or desired end-state that was pursued with that action (i.e., which action-effect was engendered by a categorical action). In fact, theoretical accounts of action control hold that actions are represented in terms of their sensory effects, which encompass both features of the kineticism, but additionally features of an action‘s effect in the world (Hommel, Müsseler, Aschersleben, Prinz, 2001; Potencies, 1973). This view suggests that gregarious-affective consequences of imitation should not be constrained to situations in which the imitator copies the model‘s body forms of kineticism. The present study corroborates this reasoning and shows that the reproduction of action-effects engendered by another person has propitious convivial consequences even when the engendering forms of kineticism are dissimilar.

1.1 Imitation in Child Development

Typically-developing children learn to imitate in infancy. If you visually examine a baby and his mother interacting, you will likely visually perceive both baby and mother imitating each other‘s sounds, actions, and countenances. This back-and-forth imitation is genuinely an early conversation without words, and it avails infants learn to express interest in their caregiver for convivial reasons (as opposed to expressing rudimentary needs like pabulum or slumber), share an emotion with their caregiver and take turns fixate on their caregiver.

Children use imitation throughout infancy and early childhood to have gregarious exchanges with their caregivers and to learn incipient things. Infants first imitate their caregiver‘s actions with toys and objects, and they then go on to imitate gestures during the second year of life. Toddlers interact by replicating each other’s actions with toys, and this kind of imitation increases throughout early childhood.

“Imitation is vital to the development of abilities ranging from language to social skills,” explains Lisa Nalven, M.D., a developmental and behavioral pediatrician at the Valley Center for Child Development, in Ridgewood, New Jersey. But not all children jump in and mimic their parents' every move. “Some children spend a lot of time observing and processing information before they attempt something,” says Daniel B. Kessler, M.D., director of developmental and behavioral pediatrics at the Children's Health Center of St. Joseph's Hospital, in Phoenix.

1.2 Aristotle’s Theory of Imitation

Plato was the first to use the word “imitation” in cognation with poetry, but Aristotle breathed into it an incipient definite construal. So poetic imitation is no longer considered mimicry, but is regarded as an act of imaginative engenderment by which the poet, drawing his material from the phenomenal world, makes something incipient out of it.

In Aristotle's view, principle of imitation amalgamates poetry with other fine arts and is the mundane substructure of all the fine arts. It thus differentiates the fine arts from the other category of arts. While Plato equated poetry with painting, Aristotle equates it with music. It is no longer a servile depiction of the appearance of things, but it becomes a representation of the passions and emotions of men which are withal imitated by music. Thus Aristotle by his theory enlarged the scope of imitation. The poet imitates not the surface of things but the authenticity embedded within. In the very first chapter of the Poetic, Aristotle verbally expresses:

Epic poetry and Tragedy, Comedy withal and Dithyrambic poetry, as withal the music of the flute and the lyre in most of their forms, are in their general conception modes of imitation. They differ however, from one another in three reverences – their medium, the objects and the manner or mode of imitation, being in each case distinct.

The medium of the poet and the painter are different. One imitates through form and colour, and the other through language, rhythm and harmony. The musician imitates through rhythm and harmony. Thus, poetry is more akin to music. Further, the manner of a poet may be pristinely narrative, as in the Epic, or depiction through action, as in drama. Even dramatic poetry is differentiated into tragedy and comedy accordingly as it imitates man as better or worse.

Aristotle verbalizes that the objects of poetic imitation are "men in action." The poet represents men as worse than they are. He can represent men better than in authentic life predicated on material supplied by history and legend rather than by any living figure. The poet culls and authoritatively mandates his material and reconstitutes authenticity. He brings order out of Chaos. The irrational or fortuitous is abstracted and attention is fixated on the lasting and the paramount. Thus he gives a veracity of an ideal kind. His mind is not tied to authenticity:

It is not the function of the poet to relate what has transpired but what may transpire – according to the laws of probability or desideratum.

History tells us what genuinely transpired; poetry what may transpire. Poetry inclines to express the ecumenical, history the particular. In this way, he exhibits the preponderation of poetry over history. The poet liberated from the tyranny of facts, takes a more immensely colossal or general view of things, represents the ecumenical in the particular and so shares the philosopher's quest for ultimate veracity.He thus equates poetry with philosophy andshows that both are designates to a higher veracity. By the word 'ecumenical' Aristotledesignates:

How a person of a certain nature or type will, on a particular occasion, verbalize or act, according to the law of probability or desideratum.

The poet perpetually elevates from the particular to the general. He studies the particular and devises principles of general application. He exceeds the constraints of life without breaching the essential laws of human nature.

Elsewhere Aristotle verbally expresses, "Art imitates Nature." By 'Nature' he does not mean the outer world of engendered things but "the ingenious force, the productive principle of the macrocosm." Art reproduce mainly an inward process, a physical energy working outwards, deeds, incidents, situation, being included under it so far as these spring from an inward, act of will, or draw some activity of mentally conceived or feeling. He renders men, "as they ought to be."

The poet imitates the ingenious process of nature, but the objects are "men in action." Now the 'action' may be 'external' or 'internal.' It may be the action within the soul caused by all that befalls a man. Thus, he brings human experiences, emotions and passions within the scope of poetic imitation. According to Aristotle's theory, moral qualities, characteristics, the sempiternal temper of the mind, the transitory emotions and feelings, are all action and so objects of poetic imitation.

Poetry may imitate men as better or worse than they are in authentic life or imitate as they genuinely are. Tragedy and epic represent men on a heroic scale, better than they are, and comedy represents men of a lower type, worse than they are. Aristotle does not discuss the third possibility. It betokens that poetry does not aim at photographic realism. In this connection R. A. Scott-James points out that:

Aristotle kenned nothing of the "authentic" or "fleshy" school of fiction – the school of Zola or of Gissing.

Abercrombie, in contrast, bulwarks Aristotle for not discussing the third variant. He verbalizes:

"It is just possible to imagine life precisely as it is, but the exhilarating thing is to imagine life as it might be, and it is then that imagination becomes an impulse capable of inspiring poetry."

Aristotle by his theory of imitation answers the charge of Plato that poetry is an imitation of "shadow of shadows," thrice abstracted from veracity, and that the poet beguiles us with lies. Plato condemned poetry that in the very nature of things poets have no conception of veracity. The phenomenal world is not the authenticity but a replica of the authenticity in the mind of the Supreme. The poet imitates the objects and phenomena of the world, which are shadowy and illusory. Poetry is, ergo, "the mother of prevarications."

Aristotle, on the contrary, tells us that art imitates not the mere shows of things, but the 'ideal authenticity' embodied in very object of the world. The process of nature is a 'ingenious process'; everywhere in 'nature there is a ceaseless and upward progress' in everything, and the poet imitates this upward kineticism of nature. Art reproduces the pristine not as it is, but as it appears to the senses. Art moves in a world of images, and reproduces the external, according to the conception or image in his mind. Thus the poet does not facsimile the external world, but engenders according to his 'conception' of it. Thus even a homely object well-imitated becomes a source of congeniality. We are told in "The Poetics":

Objects which in themselves we view with pain, we delectate to contemplate when reproduced with minute fidelity; such as the forms of the most ignoble animals and dead bodies.

The genuine and the ideal from Aristotle's perspective are not antitheses; theideal is the genuine, shorn of chance and contingency, a purified form of authenticity. And it is this higher 'authenticity' which is the object of poetic imitation. Idealization is achieved by divesting the genuine of all that is contingent, transient and particular. Poetry thus imitates the ideal and the macrocosmic; it is an "idealized representation of character, emotion, action – under forms manifest in sense." Poetic veracity, consequently, is higher than historical veracity. Poetry is more philosophical, more conducive to understanding than Philosophy itself.

Thus Aristotle prosperously and conclusively confuted the charge of Plato and provided a defence of poetry which has ever since been utilized by doters of poetry in justification of their Muse. He breathed incipient life and soul into the concept of poetic imitation and showed that it is, in authenticity, an ingenious process.

In Aristotle's view, poetic imitation is an act of imaginative creation by which the poet draws his poetic material from the phenomenal world, and makes something new out of it. Creating a new thing out of something is not its imitation, but is actually the creativity of the person who creates this new thing.

Aristotle's theory of imitation is a great landmark in the history of literary criticism. It has been accepted all over the world as a guiding principle. By declaring poetic imitation a creative process Aristotle has given poetry a very high place in the realm of Art and literature.

1.3 Don't Imitate Others Constantly

We imitate others in style, in content, and in strategy. Sometimes, we hear preachers who sound exactly like their 'hero.' They have adopted the same style, same approach, and even the same cadence in their voice as the leader they admire. Why do people do this? They might think, If I imitate a great leader, I will become a great leader. Well, yes and no. Learning and getting inspired from great leaders can make you a better leader. Constantly imitating other leaders can actually do damage. Imitating often enough means killing something God-given inside.

Chances are the person you are imitating didn't become a great leader by mimicking someone else. Far more likely, they developed the gifts God gave them to their fullest potential, which leads us to the first problem with the constant imitation of leaders:

- Envying someone else's gift will cause you to neglect your own.
- It will do other things that will permanently hamper your leadership if you are not careful.

1.4 Imitation is NOT Bad Always

Imitation isn't always a bad thing. Thereare times when it is simply prudent and expedient to imitate. Here are a few examples:

- When someone else has done something better than you and you have permission to use their material, strategy, or approach.
- When someone discovers a smarter, faster way to complete a task.
- No one in your team is creative enough to design a better mouse trap.

In such cases, imitation can be beneficial. And, of course, it's a good idea to emulate the best practises of great leaders. However, persistent imitation goes muchdeeper than that. That is why it is lethal.

1.5 Literary Imitation

Literary imitation can be thought about in a similar way i.e., learning by imitating other people. When someone imitates an earlier text, they are not necessarily just taking words from that text. Indeed, the object of literary imitation is usually not simply a sequence of words, but something much more nebulous: a style, or a way of writing. A later author can learn a style from an earlier author—as Keats did from Edmund Spenser, for instance—or a way of structuring sentences, or a stanzaic form. Literary imitation, that is, does not have to be about verbal replication. It can be a means by which writers learn from the past how to do something new.

People learn how to do things by closely watching how others do it, by practicing the skills they see in others, and by working out new ways of achieving similar outcomes. Literary imitation can be very similar. The pressure to be original and creative and to avoid the stigma of producing "a thing made to look like something else," puts pressure on writers to avoid dependency on other creative agents.

1.6 Constant Imitation KILLS Innovation

People who constantly imitate rarely innovate. Imitate long enough, and imitate hard enough, and there won't be much innovation left in you or your organization. Constant imitation means you will rarely take risks. It means you will wait for someone else to blaze trails. Imitators are always one,two or five steps behind. They have to wait for the next product, approach or strategy tobe revealed. Then they madly copy. If you are always imitating, your trajectory will never be greater than the person you are copying. Ever. It will always be a shadow of theirs.

There are sundry edifying learning processes practiced in schools. Some of these impart imitation learning and others a real learning.

Imitation learning occurs when the child does not understand the concept as it is and so cannot apply learning to other processes and systems of life. Imitation learning is for pretending to ken enough to illude the examiner, so that an examination is passed. Imitation learning aims for a concrete exam prosperity. It is half baked cognizance, forgotten after the exam. Imitation learning is fictitious potentiation, without having the authentic vigor. This type of learning will never make a child creative and innovative.

Real learning is development of skills, independence of cerebrating and incipient learning with initiative for enquiry, responsibility, self-management and convivial skills as components of the design of the curriculum. Real learning involves all the senses and links the words in the book with the genuine life experiments, models, activities etc. It is the building of understanding, skills and postures which is genuine potentiation of the child for perennial prosperity. Real learning is education for life. This type of learning develops creativity and innovativeness in a child.

1.7 Constant Imitation versus Creativity

If your creative meetings essential consist of "what did so and so do?" and then adapting it to your service, you are not very creative. I totally believe wisdom hasmany counselors, and I learn from a ton of people and a ton of organizations. But, there is a world of difference between spring boarding off others and relying on others to think for you. True creativity is risky. It means you don't know how it will turn out. It means you have to trust God and trust your judgment.

When an imitator is called-upon to explain their process or provide directions or instructions they can't produce. The critical thinking that goes into the creative process was bypassed – skipped right over – and all the details and moments of frustration or success don't exist and can't be fabricated.

This can also show up in their work, if theyrushed too quickly, missed important steps,or produced poor quality work because shortcuts were taken. Creativity grows through learning skills from others. We should not regard it as paradoxical to claimthat creativity is the product of imitation.

When imitators encounter problems, they often don't know how to get around them. An imitator while trying to change the copy of the text in the project, it all goes loopy and the imitator has no idea how to fixit. That is when an imitator has to put their tail between their legs, admit they are shortcoming, and ask for help – or, risk failing and losing the project, altogether.

1.8 Ways to STOP Imitating Others

When we opt to emulate someone else in lieu of being who we are, we are telling God that he was erroneous in engendering us the way he has. God doted you and made you different than everyone else. No one will ever be you. Embrace who you are.

Every person has a plethora of strengths and impotencies. The primary goal is to identify them. When you endeavor to be someone else, you are ignoring the forces that lie within yourself. The person you are endeavoring to imitate is not better than you, but they are different, and that is okay.

Everyone has a different experience than others. Imitating other people is fruitless because you will never plenarily follow them because their experiences are unique to them. You could never be me, and I could never be you. We are different in so many ways, and that fact is a comely thing.

Rather than endeavoring to facsimile somebody we should endeavor to discover ourselves, understand out veritable nature and endeavor to be ourselves. Let's discover genuine us. Let us give us a chance to expressour veritable self. Let us just be ourself.

2. The Second 'I': Inspiration

Inspiration is derived from the Latin word *inspirare*, meaning "to breathe into" is an unconscious burst of creativity in a literary, musical, or visual art and other artistic endeavours. The concept has origins in both Hellenism and Hebraism. The Greeks believed that inspiration or "enthusiasm" came from the muses, as well as the gods Apollo and Dionysus. Similarly, in the Ancient Norse religions, inspiration derives from the gods, such as Odin.

The Oxford Dictionary defines inspiration as:

"The process of being mentally stimulated to do or feel something, especially to do something creative."

Commonly, we cerebrate of people being arbitrarily struck by a flash of inspiration, so we visually perceive inspiration as a feeling that occurs virtually by contingency. However, as the commencement of that dictionary definition states, inspiration is a process. We become mentally stimulated (inspired) to do something. For those who want to feel inspired, the key is to learn how to engender an inspired state when we require to.

Inspiration is a motivational state that compels individuals to bring conceptions into fruition. Engenderers have long argued that inspiration is consequential to the ingenious process, but until recently, scientists have not investigated this claim. In this article, we review challenges to the study of ingenious inspiration, as well as solutions to these challenges afforded by theoretical and empirical work on inspiration over the past decennium. A better understanding of the biological substructure of inspiration will illuminate the process through which ingenious conceptions "fire the soul," such that individuals are compelled to transform conceptions into products and solutions that may benefit society.

Describing his creative process, Mozart observed, "Those ideas that please me I retain in memory, and am accustomed, as I have been told, to hum them to myself. If I continue in this way," he writes, "it soon occurs to me how I may turn this or that morsel to account so as to make a good dish of it… All this fires my soul" (Harding, 1948). Mozart's depiction of inspiration possesses all of the core elementsof the modern scientific inspiration construct—appreciation of new or better possibilities ("ideas that please me"), passive evocation ("it…occurs to me"), and motivation to bring the new possibilities into fruition (turning a morsel into a dish; "fires my soul"). Like Mozart, writers, artists, and other creators commonly emphasize the importance of inspiration in the creative process (Harding, 1948). Despite this, until recently, scientists have given little attention to inspiration.

Perhaps, it is not surprising that inspiration has received little attention within the scientific community, given the numerous challenges that the inspiration concept has presented. Among these challenges have been (a) a lack of clarity about the meaning of inspiration; (b) difficulty of operationalization; (c) ambiguity about whether inspiration is distinct from related constructs; (d) preconceptions that inspiration is not an important relative to "perspiration," and (e) a variety of barriers to neuroscientific investigation. Let me address each of these challenges and point to opportunities for expanding upon the emerging scientific literature on inspiration.

2.1/ (a) Conceptualization

The term "inspiration" has been used in a variety disciplines (e.g., erudite review, theology, psychology) and literatures within psychology (e.g., social comparison, humanism, creative process). Frequently the term isn't defined, is used interchangeably with other constructs, or is substantiated only to be critiqued as fabulous, insignificant, or unscientific. Farther complicating matters, inspiration historically has been studied in a sphere-specific manner, with little communication between experimenters across disciplines. Feting the need for a unified, integrated description of the inspiration construct, Thrash and Elliot (2003, 2004) shouldered the task of developing a sphere-general conceptualization that drew upon the core similarities across different literatures. These sweats have yielded three reciprocal fabrics for conceptualizing inspiration that concentrate on different aspects of construct description core characteristics, element processes, and the transmission model. In this section, we review these sphere-generalconceptualizations and also show how they may be applied specifically to the case of inspiration to produce.

2.2 Tripartite Conceptualization

The tripartite conceptualization (Thrash and Elliot, 2003) specifies the three core characteristics of the state of inspiration: evocation, preponderancy, and approach provocation. Evocation refers to the fact that alleviation is elicited rather than initiated volitionally by the existent. In other words, bone doesn't feel directly responsible for getting inspired; rather, a encouragement object, similar as a person, an idea, or a work of art, evokes and sustains the inspiration occasion. During an occasion of inspiration, the individual earnings mindfulness of new possibilities that transcend ordinary or mundane enterprises. The new mindfulness is pictorial and concrete, and it surpasses the ordinary constraints of consciously generated ideas.

Once inspired, the individual gets a compelling approach provocation to transmit, appear, or express the new vision. This set of three characteristics is intended to be minimally sufficient to distinguish the state of inspiration from other countries.

2.3 Element Processes

Inspiration may be conceptualized not only in terms of the characteristics of the inspired state, but also in terms of the temporally and functionally distinct processes that compose an occasion of inspiration. Thrash and Elliot (2004) argued that inspiration involves two distinct processes — a fairly unresistant process that they called being inspired by, and a fairly active process that they called being inspired to. The process of being inspired by involves appreciation of the perceived natural value of a encouragement object, whereas the process of being inspired to involves provocation to appear or extend the valued rates to a new object. For illustration, one might be inspired by a stirring daylight, or by the fineness of a new idea that arrives during an sapience or "aha" moment. Later one might be inspired to makeup or shoulder a new exploration design. The existent can, at any time look to (or recall) the eliciting encouragement for motivational food. Thrash and Elliot (2004) further proposed that the process of being inspired by gives rise to the core characteristics of evocation and preponderancy, whereas the process of being inspired to gives rise to the core specific of approach provocation.

These element processes are posited to be present across different instantiations of inspiration. Thrash and Elliot (2004) asked actors to produce narratives recalling either a time when they were inspired or a birth experience (control condition). The inspiration narratives gauged motifs similar as getting amped by a scientific or cultural sapience, discovering one's calling, being told by a part model to succeed or live innocently, and realizing that greatness is possible in response to an unanticipated success. Despite superficial differences in narrative content, the inspiration narratives participated the underpinning themes of having one's eyes opened during an hassle with a person, object, event, or idea (i.e., being inspired "by"), and wishing to express or appear one's new vision (i.e., being inspired "to").

2.4 Transmission Model

From a lower descriptive and more theoretical viewpoint, inspiration may be conceptualized in terms of its purpose or function (Thrash and Elliot, 2004; Thrash etal., 2010b). Whereas simpler forms of approach provocation serve the function of movement toward and attainment of asked thing objects (e.g., food or cooperation), inspiration is posited to serve a unique approach function it motivates the transmission or expression of the recently appreciated rates of the eliciting object (Thrash and Elliot, 2004; Thrash etal., 2010b). Inspiration, therefore, serves the part of a middleman in a statistical sense. For case, certain merits that one observes in another person may lead to inspiration, which, in turn, leads the inspired existent to pursue these same merits in a unborn tone. Also, a creative seminal idea may inspire theindividual, compelling him or her to bring the idea into consummation in the form of a creative invention, lyric, or other palpable product.

2.5 Inspiration to Produce

The general inspiration construct as

conceptualized over may be applied directly to the specific sphere of creative exertion. From the perspective of the triplex conceptualization, the general specific of preponderancy takes the form of creativity— the new or better possibilities are appreciated specifically for their creative eventuality. Regarding the element process conceptualization, the process of being inspired by is urged by the emergence of creative ideas in knowledge, frequently during a moment of sapience. Under optimal conditions (e.g., if the idea is practicable, and the person has the capacity for approach provocation), the process of being inspired by gives way to the process of being inspired to, which motivates action. Regarding the transmission model, creative inspiration frequently takes a specific form of transmission called fruition (Thrash etal., 2010b), in which one is inspired to bring a creative idea into consummation (i.e., the desirable features of the elicitor are transmitted from a seminal idea to a completed product).

We emphasize that, according to our conceptualization, inspiration isn't posited to be the source of creative ideas. Rather, inspiration is a motivational response to creative ideas. Therefore, inspiration explains the transmission, not the origin, of creativity. This distinction is critical for at least three reasons. First, claiming that creativity comes from inspiration would not prop scientific understanding, important as attributing creativity to a "poet" would be an exercise in labeling a mysterious cause, not a scientific explanation. Second, scientists have formerly developed a variety of scientific constructs and propositions to explain the origins of creative ideas, which include situational, dispositional, tone-nonsupervisory, cognitive, literal, and neurological processes (e.g., Koestler, 1964; Rothenberg, 1979; Martindale, 1990; Finke etal., 1992; Sternberg and Davidson, 1995; Amabile, 1996; Feist, 1998; Bowden and Jung-Beeman, 2003; Simonton, 2003; Baas etal., 2013). In discrepancy, scientists have given fairly little attention to the processes through which creative ideas are converted into creative products. The inspiration construct helps fill this gap in the exploration literature. Eventually, because this conceptualization of creative inspiration is deduced from a general conceptualization, it's harmonious with operation of the inspiration construct in other literatures. For case, creative inspiration is a response to (not the cause of) creative ideas, much as interpersonal inspiration is a response to (not the cause of) righteous rates in others.

2.6/ (b) Operationalization

Given the personal nature and elusiveness of the experience of inspiration, how can it possibly be quantified in the laboratory? One might be tempted to throw up one's hands and turn instead to something that is more amenable to direct experimental control.

2.7 The Value of Self-Report

We maintain that self-report is a straightforward and congruous method for operationalizing inspiration, because the inspiration construct is inextricably intertwined with a distinctive phenomenological experience. Numerous engenderers have claimed—through conscious self-reports—that they experience inspiration and that this experience is critical to their ingenious process (Harding, 1948). Operationalizing inspiration through self-report sanctions researchers to put such claims to the test.

Thrash and Elliot (2003) developed a

trait measure of called the Inspiration Scale (IS). Albeit the term "trait" has a variety of connotations, trait inspiration refers to nothing other than individual differences in the proclivity to experience the state of inspiration. Because inspiration is a construct that is paramount in individuals' lives but underappreciated by psychologists, the quantification was designed to be straightforward and face valid. Items include verbalizations such as, "Something I encounter or experience inspires me" and "I am inspired to do something." The IS has two internally consistent 4-item subscales: inspiration frequency and intensity. Both subscales are internally consistent, with Cronbach's αs equipollent to or more preponderant than 0.90. The two subscales have been demonstrated to be highly correlated (r = 0.60 to 0.80), and ergo scores may be summed to compose an internally consistent 8-item index of overall inspiration. The IS demonstrates quantification invariance across time (2 months) and across populations (patent holders, university alumni), denoting that the underlying latent constructs have commensurable meaning at different points in time and in different populations. Two-month test-retest reliabilities for both subscales are high, r =0.77. In short, the IS has excellent psychometric properties. Eminently, the intensity subscale has been acclimated forutilize as a state measure (e.g., Thrash and Elliot, 2004; Thrash et al., 2010a).

Some may worry that self-reported inspiration cannot be trusted, that it is not objective, or that it does not provide a full explication. We respond to each of these potential circumscriptions. First, inspiration, as assessed with the IS, inclines to be unrelated or impotently cognate to gregarious desirability, and its predictive validity is robust when gregarious desirability is controlled1 (Thrash and Elliot, 2003; Thrash et al., 2010a). Second, albeit the IS provides a subjective designator of inspiration, scores on this quantification have been linked to a variety of external criteria and objective outcomes, as reviewed in the following section. Moreover, consciousness plays a critical role in the simulation of future action in humans (Baumeister and Masicampo, 2010) and may be obligatory for inspired action. Accordingly, conscious self-report is intrinsically congruous to the construct.

Conclusively, we agnize that self-report measures may leave some researchers with a hunger for lower-level explications, such as those involving physiological or neurological processes, but we optically discern this as an opportunity rather than a problem—the inspiration construct may visually perceive an exhilarating second generation of research regarding neural underpinnings. In this case, self-reported inspiration provides a "bootstrap" that may guide researchers to underlying process. Albeit it is veritable that the self-report method is circumscribed in some ways, it offers a well-validated starting point for neuroscientific investigations. Moreover, notinvestigating inspiration on the grounds that it is quantified by self-report would lead researchers to overlook a critical soothsayer of ingenious output, the biological underpinnings of which would remain undiscovered.

2.8 The Place of Inspiration in Ingenuity Research Paradigms

The field of ingenuity assessment is active and dynamic, and thus a review of the literature is well beyond the scope of this article (for a review, visually perceive

Plucker and Makel, 2010). We note, however, that the ascendant research paradigms utilized in the study of ingenuity have unwittingly precluded attention to inspiration. Ingeniousness is most often assessed utilizing tests of ingenious ideation (e.g., Alternate Uses) or ingenious insight (e.g., Remote Associates Test). While such tests are very practical in laboratory contexts and sanction researchers to fixate on the processes underlying the emergence of ingenious conceptions, they do not sanction participants to transform ingenious conceptions into ingenious products. Failure to accommodate the conception actualization process—that is, creation per se—renders inspiration speciously immaterial to the ingenious process. If the function of inspiration within the context of ingeniousness is the actualization of ingenious conceptions into ingenious products, utilizable paradigms must sanction for conception actualization. Product-predicated assessments, such as the Consensual Assessment Technique (FELINE; Amabile, 1982) and analysis of patent data, are the gold standard if one wishes to investigate the unique contribution of inspiration to the ingenious process. In fact, pertinence to inspiration aside, assessment of ingenious products is considered by some to be the most congruous and valid operationalization of ingeniousness (Baer et al., 2004; Baer and McKool, 2009).

2.9/ (c) Discriminant Validity

Ambiguity about whether inspiration is distinct from other constructs has been another impediment to research activity. If one postulates that inspiration is identically tantamount thing as, for example, ingenuity or insight, then one has no reason to study it. In this section, we elucidate the distinctions between inspiration and several other constructs (ingenuity, insight, and positive affect).

2.10 Inspiration and Ingeniousness

While there is considerable variability in the definition and utilization of the term ingeniousness within psychology (Silvia and Kaufman, 2010), there is some degree of consensus that ingeniousness implicatively insinuates two qualities: novelty and usefulness (e.g., Feist, 1998; Plucker et al., 2004). We find it serviceable to explicitly conceptualize ingeniousness as an appraisal of novelty and usefulness that may be applied to any of a variety of objects, categorically conceptions and resulting products. Depending on the aims of the research, this appraisal may be made by the engenderer herself, by gatekeepers within a field, by an audience, or through sundry other operationalizations available to the researcher. We note that researchers often appear to have either conceptions or products in mind as the ultimate objects of ingenuity appraisals, even when the term "creative" precedes other entities (e.g., ingenious activity (Simonton, 2000), ingenious insights (Csikszentmihalyi and Sawyer, 1995), ingenious personalities (Feist, 2010), ingenious states (Jamison, 1989), or ingenious processes (Kris, 1952)).

Albeit the terms inspiration and ingeniousness have infrequently been used synonymously (e.g., Schuler, 1994; Chamorro-Premuzic, 2006), our conceptualizations of inspiration and ingenuity involve a clear delineation. Ingeniousness is an appraisal of novelty and usefulness that may apply (to sundry degrees) to content at any point in the ingenious process, from a seminal conception to the consummated product. Inspiration, in contrast, is a motivational state. We posit that inspiration is often elicited when an engenderer appraises his or her conception as ingenious, and it is posited to incentivize actualization of the conception in the form of a product that is likewise appraised (by its engenderer and perhaps others) as ingenious. We discuss empirical support for these proposals below.

2.11 Inspiration and Insight

Conflation of inspiration with insight is prevalent in everyday language. An individual might exclaim, "I had an inspiration," where "inspiration" refers to the conception itself, not to the motivational replication. In the scientific context, the term insight has been used to describe the process by which a quandary solver suddenly peregrinates from a state of not kenning how to solve a quandary to a state of kenning how to solve it (Mayer, 1992). Within the ingenuity context, insight has additionally been conceptualized as the cognitive content that enters consciousness suddenly; the "aha!" moment (Csikszentmihalyi and Sawyer, 1995). Regardless of its exact utilization, insight can be differentiated from inspiration in terms of its theoretical function. Whereas insight research is an endeavor to expound the cognitive mechanisms, such as restructuring (Ohlsson, 1984), by which conceptions enter vigilance, inspiration research is an endeavor to expound the motivational replication that often (but not always) follows ingenious insight (visually perceive Thrash et al., 2010b).

If inspiration always followed from insight, then perhaps the inspiration construct would be superfluous. However, inspiration does not always follow. Thrash et al. (2010b) found that ingenious ideation inclines to lead to inspiration but that this effect is mitigates by individuals approach temperament (i.e., sensitivity to reward; Elliot and Thrash, 2010). Individuals' with avigorous approach temperament incline to get inspired to engender in replication to ingenious insight, whereas individuals with an impuissant approach temperament report feeling a lack of inspiration in spite of their insight. Inspiration thus has consequential implicative insinuations for the behavioral transmission of an ingenious insight into an ingenious product.

Recent work on the phenomenology of insight offers hints about how insight may lead to inspiration. Abrupt transmutations in processing fluency during insight have been found to endow an individual with ascended levels of positive affect (PA) and perceived veracity regarding his or her solution (Topolinski and Reber, 2010). Given that PA is involved in both the insight "aha" experience and inspiration, it may facilitate a fluid transition from insight to inspiration. Moreover, perceiving one's solution as veritable, a consequence of insight, may bolster inspired motivation. As we have noted, however, insight can occur without inspiration. Dispositional factors of the individual (e.g., low approach temperament) and circumstantial factors (e.g., contexts in which opportunities for transmission are not available) can impede inspiration. Likewise, inspiration can occur outside of the quandary-solving context and without a discrete and sudden insight.

2.12 Inspiration and Positive Affect

Activated PA, a high-arousal form of congenial affect, is the most vigorous kenned correlate of inspiration (Thrash and Elliot, 2003). Indeed, the term "inspired" appears on the PANAS measure of activated PA (Watson et al., 1988). Because activated PA is often present during states of approach motivation (Watson et al., 1999), it categorically resembles the inspired to component process.

Albeit inspiration and activated PA overlap to some degree empirically and conceptually, considerable evidence fortifies their discriminant validity. First, inspiration and activated PA are factorially distinct (Thrash and Elliot, 2003). Second, consistent with the tripartite conceptualization of inspiration, experiences of inspiration involve more preponderant levels of transcendence and lower calibers of volitional control and ascriptions of personal responsibility (indicative of "evocation" compared to experiences of activated PA (Thrash and Elliot, 2004). Third, inspiration and activated PA have different proximal and distal antecedents (Thrash and Elliot, 2004). Activated PA is triggered proximally by reward salience (environmental cues and perceptions that something desired is attainable) and distally by approach temperament. In contrast, inspiration is triggered proximally by experiences of insight and distally by openness to experience. Determinately, inspiration and activated PA have different distributions across days of the week; on Fridays, for instance, activated PA is at its peak while inspiration is at its trough (Thrash, 2007).

2.13/ (d) Inspiration, Perspiration andIngeniousness

Perhaps the most pernicious obstruction to research on inspiration has been the longstanding notion that it is perspiration, and not inspiration, that is critical for ingenious output. Thomas Edison, regarding his work, once remarked that, "what it boils down to is one per cent inspiration and ninety-nine per cent perspiration" (Edison, 1903). This comment has sometimes been offered in support of the conception that effort is consequential to ingenuity and that inspiration, by comparison, is nugatory (e.g., Martindale, 1989, 2001; Sawyer, 2006).

Furthering this line of reasoning, Fehrman and Petherick (1980) offered an account of why inspiration nonetheless endures as a folk explication of ingeniousness: when individuals are exposed to ingenious works, they misattribute creators' effort to inspiration, incognizant how much effort was required to engender the work. It appears that reasoning such as this has precluded attention to a legitimate role of inspiration in the ingenious process.

Empirical data cognate to inspiration, perspiration, and ingenuity are now available for consideration. A number of studies betokens that inspiration is a robust prognosticator of ingeniousness. At the between-person (i.e., trait) level, inspiration and ingenious self-concept are positively correlated, and inspiration presages longitudinal increases in ingenious self-concept (Thrash and Elliot, 2003). Trait inspiration withal presages objective bespeakers of ingenious output. In a sample of U.S. patent holders, inspiration frequency was found to prognosticate the number of patents held (Thrash and Elliot, 2003). Inspiration withal presages ingeniousness atthe within-person level, such that inspiration and self-reported ingenuity fluctuatetogether across days (Thrash and Elliot, 2003).

In three studies of variants of inscribing (poetry, science, and fiction), self-reported state inspiration during the inditement process uniquely prognosticated ingeniousness of the final product, as assessed by expert judges utilizing the FELINE (Thrash et al., 2010b). These findings held when a variety of covariates (e.g., openness to experience, effort, activated PA, awe) were controlled. Determinately, inspiration has been shown to mediate between the ingenuity of seminal conceptions and the ingeniousness of final products in a manner consistent with the posited transmission function4 of inspiration (Thrash et al., 2010b). Covariates of inspiration (effort, activated PA, awe) failed to mediate transmission, denoting that the transmission function is unique to inspiration.

Having established a cognation between inspiration and ingeniousness, we now consider the role of "perspiration" in the ingenious process. Eminently, Thrash et al.

(2010b) documented a positive cognition, rather than a negative cognation, between inspiration and effort, betokening that these constructs are not mutually exclusive as the Edison quote may implicatively insinuate. The postulation that the presence of effort designates low calibers of inspiration is further challenged by a positive cognation between inspiration and the work-mastery component of desideratum for achievement (Thrash and Elliot, 2003). Both of these findings were documented at two statistically independent levels of analysis (between-persons, within-persons).

Certainly effort is consequential to the ingenious process, but its role is different than that of inspiration. Whereas writers' inspiration prognosticates the ingenuity of the product, writers' effort prognosticates the technical merit of the product (Thrash et al., 2010b). Thus inspiration and effort are unique prognosticators of different aspects of product quality. Moreover, screen capture data designate that inspiration is involved in the automatic/generative aspects of the inscription process (e.g., inspired writers engender more words and retain more of their pristine inditing), whereas effort is cognate to controlled self-regulation (e.g., writers who exert effort expunge more words and pause more to cerebrate; Thrash et al., 2010b). In short, inspiration and "perspiration" are not mutually exclusive, and they contribute in qualitatively different ways to the ingenious process and product.

The question of whether the audience felicitously infers the presence of inspiration remains. The misattribution hypothesis states that it is the creator's effort that presages the ingenuity of the product but that the audience erroneously attributes this ingenuity to inspiration in the engenderer. An alternative to this model is the possibility that the audience congruously infers inspiration (Bowra, 1977). Thrash et al. (2010b) tested these competing hypotheses. Readers were found to opportunely attribute ingenuity to writers' inspiration; likewise, they congruously attributed technical merit to writers' effort. These results, in additament to providing the first empirical evidence that readers can make veridical inferences about writers' motivational states, denote that folk notions of the paramountcy of inspiration are borne out by empirical data.

The psychological science of inspiration, as well as its cognation to ingenuity, is now well-established. Inspiration has been conceptualized through integration of usages in diverse literatures, operationalized utilizing a well-validated measure, discriminated from cognate constructs, and linked to ingeniousness in multiple populations, contexts, and levels of analysis. Prior work provides a solid substratum on which investigations into the neuroscience of inspiration can repose.

2.14/ (e) Inspiration in the NeuroscienceLaboratory

In most venerations, the challenges associated with studying ingenious inspiration are homogeneous regardless of whether one approaches the topic as a neuroscientist, a psychologist, etc. Ergo, the preceding general challenges and solutions are withal germane categorically in the neuroscience context. However, we reiterate the paramountcy of attending conscientiously to construct definition, because the term "inspiration" has infrequently been utilized in the neuroscience literature to refer to constructs that are quite different than the inspiration construct that we have discussed. In their classic EEG studies of the ingenious process, for instance, Martindale and Hasenfus (1978) utilized the terms inspiration and elaboration to refer to the stages that precede and follow, respectively, ingenious insight (visually perceive Kris, 1952, for a precedent for such utilization in psychoanalysis). Inspiration as we have defined it—i.e., as a conscious motivational state rather than as a stage—is more liable to occur during Martindale and Hasenfus's elaboration stage than during the inspiration stage. We now turn to challenges that are concretely germane within a neuroscience context.

One obstruction in studying inspiration in the laboratory is the infeasibility of direct manipulation through exposure to exogenous elicitors. If one seeks to elicit inspiration through utilization of some kind of "inspiring" stimulus, then the manipulated elicitor is the independent variable and inspiration is a dependent variable. Thus caution is needed regarding causal inference, despite utilization of the experimental method (Thrash et al., 2010a). Albeit inspiration cannot be directly manipulated through exposure to exogenous stimuli, a researcher may build a case for causality utilizing manipulation of elicitors in cumulation with statistical controls and cross-lagged analyses, as demonstrated by Thrash et al. (2010a). We note that these quandaries are not unique to the study of inspiration. Emotions, insight, and many other constructs elude stringent experimental control; at best, they may be "elicited" rather than "manipulated."

A cognate challenge is that it may be arduous to capture authentic or profound experiences of inspiration in a laboratory setting, given that inspiration is elusive for certain individuals or under certain circumstances. One solution may be to, in effect, lower the threshold for what constitutes an episode of inspiration. Thrash and Elliot (2004), for instance, studied "daily inspiration" utilizing experience sampling methods, and we suggest that such tolerance for less profound manifestations of inspiration can be elongated to a laboratory study. Much as ingeniousness is not identically tantamount thing as genius (Bruner, 1962), inspiration is a matter of degree, and moderate levels might be achievable even in some invasive neuroscience paradigms.

A third challenge is the desideratum for repeatable tribulations and time-locking. Encephalon imaging techniques (e.g., fMRI, EEG, MEG) require designs in which the phrenic event under consideration may be (a) temporally isolated so that the recorded data and the noetic event can be time-locked to an eliciting stimulus and (b) elicited perpetually during a recording session in order to amend the signal-to-noise ratio (Dickter and Kieffaber, 2013). One possible method to address these requisites is to utilize participant self-report (betokening the onset of inspiration) as the time-locking event. Suppose, for example, participants invent captions for each of a series of photographs (a highly-repeatable activity) and report on levels of inspiration at the moment of getting a conception for each caption. Bowden and Jung-Beeman (2007) utilized a method homogeneous to this in order to identify processes that distinguish solutions involving the experience of insight from those that do not. We caution, however, that inspiration generally is more protracted in time than is insight (categorically when considerable activity is needed to actualize a conception), and consequently methods that capture subsequent variability in inspiration across time—not just the caliber of inspiration at the moment of insight—will be categorically valuable.

One such method for capturing variability in inspiration across time, while simultaneously truncating the encumbrance of eliciting inspiration perpetually, is to record electrical encephalon activity utilizing a non-invasive technique (such as EEG) during the ingenious process. For instance, if researchers record screen capture data during the inditement process as in Thrash et al. (2010b), they can subsequently play back the recording to participants and accumulate perpetual measures of recalled inspiration during the ingenious process (e.g., utilizing a dial or slider input contrivance). These ebbs and flows of inspiration can then be linked to variability in neural processes.

The difficulties associated with eliciting inspiration in order to study it at the within-person level may supplementally be addressed by simply fixating on the individuals who are liable to be inspired (i.e., those who are high in trait inspiration). Elicitation may be circumvented altogether by examining structural encephalon distinctions between groups kenned to be high versus low in trait inspiration. One may separate groups into "more inspired" and "less inspired" utilizing the IS. Supplementally, as individuals higher in trait inspiration incline to exhibit more preponderant levels of openness and extraversion, one might expect, for example, truncated latent inhibition and incremented activity in the ventral tegmental area dopamine projections (Ashby et al., 1999; Depue and Collins, 1999; Peterson et al., 2002) for these individuals. Thus, inspiration's nomological network can accommodate as an informative starting point for between-person neurological analyses.

Next, we consider the question of where to look in the nervous system. While at present there is no neuroscience of the inspiration construct per se, literatures on cognate constructs can offer us some hints.

Insight relates to inspiration within the tripartite conceptualization in terms of both evocation and transcendence, and within the component processes model as the initial event that often leads one to become inspired by. During “Aha!” moments, one transcends a phrenic set and experiences a conceptual expansion (Abraham et al., 2012), and the experience feels automatic and unexpected; it feels evoked (Bowden et al., 2005). Consequently, certain neural components involved in insight experiences may be present at the onset of an inspiration episode. However, given that the literature on the neural correlates of insight is involute and that neural processes are under debate (Dietrich and Kanso, 2010), we caution against relying too heavily upon any one finding in guiding work on inspiration.

As inspiration involves not only transcendence and evocation, but adscititiously approach motivation, we may withal look to the neuroscience literature on states of approach motivation (Elliot, 2008). There subsists a burgeoning literature on approach motivation and appetitive affect, with attention to underlying neuronal circuitry (e.g., Bradley et al., 2001; Aron et al., 2005; Junghöfer et al., 2010), subcortical reward systems (e.g., Rosenkranz and Grace, 2002; Sapient, 2004; Alcaro et al., 2007), neurotransmitters (e.g., Bassareo et al., 2002; Hoebel et al., 2008), and neurohormones (e.g., Frye and Lacey, 2001; Frye and Seliga, 2003; Frye, 2007). Findings in this area may offer suggestions for the neural underpinnings of the inspired to process.

Albeit the neurological findings regarding certain aspects of the inspiration construct can offer clues, the neural components of these pieces alone are unlikely to tell the full story. After all, we have already argued above that inspiration is not identically tantamount thing as insight or activated PA, nor is it the sum of these components. For instance, an individual could be in an appetitive motivational state at the same time that he or she gets an ingenious insight, but he or she would not be inspired if the appetitive state reflects anticipation of victualing, rather than of bringing the conception into fruition. The evoking object, in this case, the insight, does not paramountly relate to the motivational object. The critical question for neuroscience is how processes cognate to generation of ingenious conceptions recruit appetitive motivational processes, such that individuals respond to ingenious conceptions not with insouciance, but rather with a feeling of being compelled to act. How precisely does the prospect of turning a morsel into a dish fire the soul, as Mozart put it (in the aperture quotation)?

In the initial stages of research on the neurological substratum of inspiration, it may be utilizable to commence with a fixate on overall inspiration in lieu of particular aspects or component processes. Inspiration as a cumulated concept can be quantified quite efficiently utilizing the 4-item intensity subscale of the IS (Thrash and Elliot, 2004). If indispensable, inspiration could be assessed with a single item from the IS. Such items are surprisingly efficacious at capturing the full inspiration construct as we have defined it (Thrash et al., 2010b).

2.15 Inspiration versus Imitation

Inspiration, pays tribute to, builds upon and advances independently in an incipient direction igniting incipient conceptions and expanding the conversation along the way. Whereas imitation, simply seeks to take the path of least resistance, mimicking the already verbalized, slothfully reproducing the already visually perceived. Throughout history, inspiration has always been used to engender incipient things out of the old, with a little twist integrated in there. It's withal a method to give a nod to the piece that inspired the incipient engenderment, so it can be a great way of appreciating the conceptions that came afore it. Taking inspiration is generally a good and salubrious way of developing your own engenderments, because you are picking and taking samples of particular features that are desirable to you and your predilections, while leaving out any thing that might not suit you quite as well.

Imitating other people isn't always the best way to engender a sense of style of your own, and you might get disoriented in the styles of other people in lieu of developing a style that you like. This is because we're all unique in the way we are built, so naturally what works for one person might not be identically tantamount for someone else.

2.16 Situations Triggering Ingenious Inspiration

There is no single, set way to make every person feel inspired. That is because we are all different and are inspired by different things. You require to learn what works for you and one of the best ways to do this, is to cerebrate about what you were doing the last few times you felt inspired. Consider where you were and what you were doing, etc. Probe for any mundane factors and incorporate these the next time you require some inspirational conceptions or answers.

Here are just a minuscule number of situations, which trigger ingenious inspiration:

- Some people find inspiration in books.
- Some find inspiration in music.
- Some people are inspired when circumvented by nature.
- Some people grab a pad and some colouring pencils and commence doodling.
- Some people become inspired to engender, when an internal or external

deadline approaches. This one is authentically fascinating, because it shows how ingenious inspiration can indeed be self driven.

- Some find inspiration through affirmations or positive self-verbalize.
- Some find inspiration comes when they are doing some type of physical activity. For me, it's ambulating that works best.
- Some find inspiration in the design of a quotidian item. (More on that in a moment.)

And others find all of the above work to a lesser or more preponderant degree.

Inspiration is a key motivator of ingenuity. Over the past decennium, scientists have tested and found vigorous support for these claims. Encephalon-level explications of an inspiration episode can then be integrated with explications at other levels of analysis to engender a richer and more holistic understanding of inspiration. This deeper understanding will avail in determining how and why individuals sometimes feel (or do not feel) compelled to act on their ingenious conceptions.

3. The Third 'I': Innovation

The word "innovation" is derived from the Latin verb *innovare,* which means to renew. It can refer either to the act of introducing something new or to the thing itself that is introduced. In terms of commerce, it is defined in the Oxford English Dictionary as "the action of introducing a new product into the market; a product newly brought on to the market," a definition that illustrates both aspects of the word's meaning. It was once used politicallyin the sense of revolution, but now you are most likely to hear it in relation to technology, or new ways of doing something. "Innovativeness" is the property of being an innovation.

Innovation is genuinely about responding to transmute in an ingenious way. It's about engendering new ideas, conducting R&D, amending processes or revamping products and accommodations. Most innovation efforts, however, are doomed to fail; they direct focus away from what is required to prosper.

Engendering something incipient is the goal of most innovation initiatives, but incipient does not mean valuable. Incrementing the value engendered for customers should be the focus of initiatives intended to engenderbusiness magnification. Over time, entrepreneurship has become associated with creativity, the facility to develop something pristine, categorically a conception or a representation of a conception. Innovation requires ingeniousness, but innovation is more concretely the application of ingeniousness.

Innovation often takes place through the development of more-effective products, processes, services, technologies, art works or business models that innovators make available to markets, governments and society. Innovation is cognate to, but not identically tantamount to, invention: innovation is moreapt to involve the practical implementation of an invention (i.e. incipient / amended facility) to make a consequential impact in amarket or society, and not all innovations require an incipient invention.

3.1 Phases of an Innovation

An innovation (or innovation process) has five main phases:

Phase 1: Conception Generation and Mobilization

The generation stage is the commencement line for incipient conceptions. Prosperous conception generation should be fueled both by the pressure to compete and by the liberation to explore. IDEO, the product development and branding company predicated in Palo Alto, California, is a good example of an organization that emboldens prosperous conception generation by finding a balance between frolicsomeness and need.

Once an incipient conception is engendered, it passes on to the mobilization stage, wherein the conception peregrinates to a different physical or logical location. Since most inventors aren't additionally marketers, an incipient conception often needs someone other than its progenitor to move it along. This stage is vitally paramount to the progression of an incipient conception, and skipping it can delay or even sabotage the innovation process.

Phase 2: Advocacy and Screening

This stage is the time for weighing an idea's pros and cons. Advocacy and screening have to take place at the same time to weed out conceptions that lack potential without sanctioning stakeholders to repudiate conceptions impulsively solely on the substratum of their novelty. The authors found that companies had more prosperity when the evaluation process was transparent and standardized, because employees felt more comfortable contributing when they could anticipate how their conceptions would be judged. For example, one software engineer from an information technology organization verbally expressed, "One of the things I have struggled with is evaluations of my conceptions. Some of my conceptions light up fires around here, while others are squashed. Needless to verbalize, I grow skeptical when [the executives] ask for conceptions and then do not provide feedback as to why a conception was not pursued."

Phase 3: Experimentation

The experimentation stage tests the sustainability of conceptions for a particular organization at a particular time — and in a particular environment. At this stage, it's paramount to determine who the customer will be and what he or she will utilize the innovation for. With that in mind, the company might discover that albeit someone has a great conception, it is ahead of its time or just not right for a particular market. However, it's paramount not to interpret these kinds of revelations as failures — they could authentically be the catalysts of incipient and better conceptions.

Washington Mutual Inc.'s recent interior redesign provides a good example of how prosperous experimentation works. In lieu of applying an incipient design to all its branches, the banking and indemnification company, headquartered in Seattle, Washington, implemented the design in just a couple of locations to optically discern how it would be received. Subsequently, when customers responded auspiciously, the bank took its innovation to the next level, applying the incipient design to several other branches. This way, the company didn't lose mazuma and time by applying an incipient conception all at once without kenning if it would prosper.

Phase 4: Commercialization

In the commercialization stage, the organization should look to its customers to verify that the innovation authentically solves their quandaries and then should analyze the costs and benefits of rolling out the innovation. The authors ascertain to note that "an invention is only considered an innovation [once] it has been commercialized." Ergo, the commercialization stage is a paramount one, homogeneous to advocacy in that it takes the right people to progress the conception to the next developmental stage. For example, one chief executive officer verbally expressed, "We learned a simple thing: Researchers and conception engenderers do not appreciate the nuances of marketing and commercialization. In the past, we endeavored to get the researchers involved in the commercialization aspects of the business. The terminus result was pain and more pain."

Phase 5: Diffusion and Implementation

The diffusion and implementation stages are, according to the authors, "two sides of the same coin." Diffusion is the process of gaining final, companywide acceptance of an innovation, and implementation is the process of establishing the structures, maintenance and resources needed to engender it. A good example of a prosperous approach to diffusion emanates from International Business Machines Corp., which involves its employees early in the conception-generation stage and conducts soi-disant innovation jams, to which they invite not only employees but withal clients, business partners and even employees' families. IBM avails later diffusion by giving everyone a stake in the conception from the commencement.

Innovative processes after phases are indispensable. This is because they create structure and systematicity to eschew mistakes and to increment the innovative performance. This ascertains that all paramount steps are consummated in a timely and redress manner. If there were no processes and phases, one would orientate without orientation perpetually back and forth rather than fixated on the goal.

3.2 Innovation Management

Innovation management, or an innovation management system, is the process of managing incipient conceptions, from ideation to taking action and making them become an authenticity. This approach has four distinct steps:

1. **Engendering:** Brainstorming and employee input to denude obnubilated concepts.

2. **Capturing:** Recording conceptions in a way that is facilely shareable with key stakeholders.

3. **Evaluating:** Discussing and reproving innovative conceptions to optically discern if they fit your desiderata.

4. **Prioritizing:** Deciding which innovative conceptions will be executed to maximize time and other resources in your company.

Innovation management informs—and is apprised by—high-level business targets that engender paramount value for your organization. Certain actions and practices will result from your innovation, just as your innovation will follow as a replication to your business vision and quandaries that arise.

In order to implement efficacious innovation management processes, you require excellent communication between employees at all levels and a collaborative environment to unearth adscititious innovative conceptions.

3.3 Innovation Strategy

Despite massive investments of management time and money, innovation remains a frustrating pursuit in many companies. Innovation initiatives frequently fail, and prosperous innovators have an arduous time sustaining their performance—as Polaroid, Nokia, Sun Microsystems, Yahoo, Hewlett-Packard, and countless others have found. Why is it so hard to build and maintain the capacity to innovate? The reasons go much deeper than the commonly cited cause: a failure to execute. The quandary with innovation amelioration efforts is rooted in the lack of an innovation strategy.

A strategy is nothing more than a commitment to a set of coherent, mutually reinforcing policies or comportments aimed at achieving a categorical competitive goal. Good strategies promote alignment among diverse groups within an organization, elucidate objectives and priorities, and avail focus efforts around them. Companies conventionally define their overall business strategy (their scope and situating) and designate how sundry functions—such as marketing, operations, finance, and R&D—will support it. But during my more than two decenniums studying and consulting for companies in a broad range of industries, I have found that firms infrequently articulate strategies to align their innovation efforts with their business strategies.

Without an innovation strategy, innovation amendment efforts can facilely become a prehension bag of much-touted best practices: dividing R&D into decentralized autonomous teams, spawning internal entrepreneurial ventures, establishing corporate venture-capital arms, pursuing external coalitions, embracing open innovation and crowdsourcing, collaborating with customers, and implementing expeditious prototyping, to denominate just a few. There is nothing erroneous with any of those practices per se. The quandary is that an organization's capacity for innovation stems from an innovation system: a coherent set of interdependent processes and structures that dictates how the company searches for novel quandaries and solutions, synthesizes conceptions into a business concept and product designs, and culls which projects get funded. Individual best practices involve trade-offs. And adopting a categorical practice generally requires a host of complementary changes to the rest of the organization‘s innovation system. A company without an innovation strategy won‘t be able to make trade-off decisions and cull all the elements of the innovation system.

Aping someone else’s system is not the answer. There is no one system that fits all companies equipollently well or works under all circumstances. There is nothing erroneous, of course, with learning from others, but it is a mistake to believe that what works for, verbally express, Apple (today’s favorite innovator) is going to work for your organization. An explicit innovation strategy avails you design a system to match your concrete competitive needs.

Determinately, without an innovation strategy, different components of an organization can facilely wind up pursuing conflicting priorities—even if there's a clear business strategy. Sales representatives aurally perceive daily about the pressing desiderata of the most immensely colossal customers. Marketing may visually perceive opportunities to leverage the brand through complementary products or to expand market share through incipient distribution channels. Business unit heads are fixated on their target markets and their particular P&L pressures. R&D scientists and engineers incline to visually perceive opportunities in incipient technologies. Diverse perspectives are critical to prosperous innovation. But without a strategy to integrate and align those perspectives around mundane priorities, the potency of diversity is blunted or, worse, becomes self-vanquishing.

A good example of how a tight connection between business strategy and innovation can drive long-term innovation leadership is found in Corning, a leading manufacturer of specialty components utilized in electronic exhibits, telecommunications systems, environmental products, and life sciences instruments. Over its more than 160 years Corning has perpetually transformed its business and grown incipient markets through breakthrough innovations. When judged against current best practices, Corning's approach seems passé. The company is one of the few with a centralized R&D laboratory (Sullivan Park, in rural upstate Incipient York). It invests a lot in fundamental research, a practice that many companies gave up long ago. And it invests heavily in manufacturing technology and plants and perpetuates to maintain a paramount manufacturing footprint in the Coalesced States, bucking the trend of wholesale outsourcing and offshoring of engenderment.

Yet when viewed through a strategic lens, Corning's approach to innovation makes perfect sense. The company's business strategy fixates on selling "keystone components" that significantly amend the performance of customers' involute system products. Executing this strategy requires Corning to be at the leading edge of glass and materials science so that it can solve exceptionally conundrums for customers and discover incipient applications for its technologies.

That requires cumbersomely hefty investments in long-term research. By centralizing R&D,

Corning ascertains that researchers from the diverse disciplinary backgrounds underlying its core technologies can collaborate. Sullivan Park has become a repository of accumulated expertise in the application of materials science to industrial quandaries. Because novel materials often require complementary process innovations, heftily ponderous investments in manufacturing and technology are a must. And by keeping a domestic manufacturing footprint, the company is able to smooth the transfer of incipient technologies from R&D to manufacturing and scale up engenderment.

Corning's strategy is not for everyone. Long-term investments in research are perilous: The telecommunications bust in the tardy 1990s devastated Corning's optical fiber business. But Corning shows the paramountcy of a limpidly articulated innovation strategy—one that's proximately linked to a company's business strategy and core value proposition. Without such a strategy, most initiatives aimed at boosting a

Firm's capacity to innovate are doomed tofail.

3.4 The Leadership Challenge

Engendering a capacity to innovate commences with strategy. The question then arises, Whose job is it to set this strategy? The answer is simple: the most senior bellwethers of the organization. Innovation cuts across just about every function. Only senior bellwethers can orchestrate such an intricate system. They must take prime responsibility for the processes, structures, aptitude, and comportments that shape how an organization searches for innovation opportunities, synthesizes conceptions into concepts and product designs, and culls what to do.

There are four essential tasks in engendering and implementing an innovation strategy. The first is to answer the question "How are we expecting innovation to engender value for customers and for our company?" and then explicate that to the organization. The second is to engender a high-level plan for allocating resources to the different kinds of innovation. Ultimately, where you spend your mazuma, time, and effort is your strategy, regardless of what you verbally express. The third is to manage trade-offs. Because every function will naturally want to accommodate its own intrigues, only senior bellwethers can make the culls that are best for the whole company.

The final challenge facing senior leadership is apperceiving that innovation strategies must evolve. Any strategy represents a hypothesis that is tested against the unfolding realities of markets, technologies, regulations, and competitors. Just as product designs must evolve to stay competitive, so too must innovation strategies. Like the process of innovation itself, an innovation strategy involves continual experimentation, learning, and adaptation.

3.5 Innovation versus Invention

People often utilize the words "invention" and "innovation" interchangeably. This is not only erroneous, but misses a few key subtleties in meaning that can transmute a conversation. Invention is about engendering something incipient, while innovation introduces the concept of "use of a conception or method." While this difference is subtle, and these words are listed in every thesaurus that I checked as synonyms of each other, they are definitely not 100% interchangeable. An invention is conventionally a "thing," while an innovation is conventionally an invention that causes vicissitude in demeanor or interactions.

Companies often claim to be a "leader in innovation" and show an astronomically immense pile of patents as evidence. Patents are evidence of inventions, of having thought of something first, and documenting the incipient invention through a licit process. The usefulness of those inventions is not proven, so "inventions" do not always equate to "innovations." There are many patents which authentically do not have a utilization or have influenced no products or industries. Patents without a "use" are not innovation.

If innovations infer the "use" of an incipient conception or method, then an invention that leads to innovation is genuinely qualified by how much it transmutes the comportments of the users, the businesses, and the processes around it.

Now perhaps the "Nose Pick" patent was a victim of deplorable marketing, poor manufacturing, or just a "right conception at the erroneous time," but conspicuously it has not transmuted demeanor and become a commonplace item in the 14 years since the patent was granted.

3.6 Innovation versus Imitation

Innovation describes how an invention is utilized in the process of engendering incipient products or accommodations. On the other hand, imitation describes how another company or person may endeavor to duplicate another's invention or innovation. The pioneers and innovators of our generation avail to shape the world we live in and their efforts are lauded by modern society. Over the centuries, ingenious ruminators were ridiculed and scorned for straying from conventional norms and branded as outlandish and even stark hazardous. However, in today's business world, innovative companies are capitalizing on that 'first mover advantage' by introducing enthusing incipient products and accommodations.

Technology gurus and business titans are proximately followed on convivial media and have become celebrities in their own right. Infelicitously, most business pioneers find themselves being imitated expeditiously by their competitors while they bear the brunt of research and development costs. Albeit imitation is a stigmatized phenomenon, there are many companies that utilize that strategy. In order to survive in this technologically competitive world, bellwethers are faced with the dilemma of adopting pioneering or imitation strategies. As ecumenical competition increases the pressure to gain and retain market share is growing.

As we have learned, a little imitation goes a long way in terms of magnification enhancing, as it promotes more frequent neck-and-neck competition and, if kept under control, does societies a world of good. What if imitative comportment becomes dysfunctional or even pathological, though, transpiring at the expense of a company's reliance on its own ingenious aptitude and vision? An exorbitant amount of imitation is by all accounts magnification minimizing or, in mathematical terms, as the facileness of imitation goes to illimitability, the magnification rate always falls to zero.

In conclusion, imitators should develop capabilities to learn more from benchmarking and imitate in a more innovative way. It may be arduous for diminutive and medium-sized businesses to pioneer given the capital required, however, local market demands may be different. By adopting a customer-centric approach and tailoring products and accommodations to the unique requisites of customers or habituating products and accommodations for novel uses, more minuscule companies can still thrive. However, duplicative imitation is insalubrious for any brand and patent rights must be reverenced. Maintaining ethical business practices are consequential for the long-term survival and reputation of every brand.

3.7 Creativity and Innovation

That most human of qualities, ingenuity evidences itself in our competency to solve challenges or quandaries with novel solutions conceptions. Shawn Hunter, author of Out Cerebrate: How Innovative Bellwethers Drive Exceptional

Outcomes (Wiley, 2013), defines ingeniousness as "the capability or act of conceiving something pristine or eccentric."

The key factor is that ingenuity remains a great conception alone, not authenticity yet. Fascinatingly, ingeniousness is very concrete to people; animals have no way to communicate involute conceptions, and much of what they do transfer is surmised by instinct or by example.

Ingeniousness and innovation, while proximately linked as a component of an engenderment process, are not equipollent. Ingeniousness isn't quantifiable, it's subjective, while innovation – at its most fundamental level meaning "incipient"– is quantifiable in the sense that an innovation is the engenderment of something incipient, whether it be an incipient product, conception or method. The cyber world never would have transpired if scientists just settled for phone lines and satellites being ample for communication. Today, we can marginally imagine functioning without digital access in just about everything we do. It took creativity and innovation to make it an authenticity.

3.8 Inspiration for Innovation

Inspiration is not something that comes facilely to everyone. Many people want to innovate and bring change to the world, but have trouble finding the motivation to keep going after some failures. Coming up with conceptions can be frolicsome, but it additionally requires a substantial magnitude of work. In order to have innovative conceptions, you should do your research first… and by research, I do not mean calculating anything or proving any hypothesis. By research, I mean inspiration! In order to come up with great conceptions, you require to get inspired. Getting inspired is not a facile task, but it is a constant effort.

Inspiring innovation seems more akin to an art than any kind of adeptness or science. The sudden spark that results in an exhilarating incipient conception seems arbitrary – like it emerged from the blue. Studies have shown what seems arbitrary was genuinely inspired by something you did, read or optically discerned in the past. Ergo, the way to more innovation is to do, read and optically discern more. Providing input to your senses as a form of fuel to your innovation effort. Fuel alone won't get your there. A car with a full fuel tank will set there without a spark of some kind. In an automobile, that spark emanates from the engine.

Inspiration for Innovation avails us to become a prosperous innovator. It offers practical insights, tips and implements and edifies you how to innovate.

Despite popular notion, inspiration doesn't just hit you one day like a tidal wave; it doesn't only transpire when you are sitting on a beach or atop a mountain. Rather, it arrives in diminutive, incremental doses, and through everyday actions and people. It must be captured and maximized. Inspiration is critical to innovation because when we feel inspired, we draw great conceptions, great people, and great energy towards us.

Different people are inspired in different ways. For some it may be reading an inspirational quote, for others it may be reviewing the progress that they have made toward their goal. Some people self-incentivize by reminding themselves of all of the people along the way that verbalized they couldn't. Conversely, others incentivize themselves by reminding themselves that someone along the way believed that they could. Whether it is a parent, a child, or a best friend, it is consequential to recollect that we are all someone's hero. That thought can accommodate as a sizably voluminous source of inspiration. It reminds us that even in our moments of self-doubt, we should optically discern ourselves as our profoundly relished ones optically discern us. The comeliness of inspiration is that it can emanate from everyday people and everyday situations. We just have to ken how and where to probe for it.

Innovators must get inspired and discover the why abaft what they optate to do. When you understand your what and can communicate your for what purport, you are yare to innovate.

Conclusion

Nature has endowed each of us with a distinct identity; we are all distinct from one another. When we try to imitate someone else, we are going against nature. Nature never duplicates; each living thing created by nature is unique. We are all unique in our own way, with our own character and qualities, but we don't even try to find them, preferring to follow someone else, and as a result, we kill our pristine self. Most of the time, when we are forced to become someone else, we lose our identity indefinitely. Our uniqueness is expressed through a smorgasbord of culls rather than specific possessions.

Imitation distorts originality and over-imitation suffocates the God-given creativity and innovativeness within. Let's get inspired from others and imitate in an innovative way i.e., to create a new thing out of something.

— Mohsin Gulzar

Our society, family, and even our parents always want us to follow some 'real' examples, which they refer to as models. Their accomplishments are admirable, and there is nothing wrong with drawing inspiration from their lives to shape our own. Our eldersalways strive to show us a prognosticable path; for example, a common cause of failure is a misconstrued zeal for the boy on the part of his parents. Such a boy is showing less interest in his studies because he is following a path determined by his parents, which contradicts all of his interestsand abilities. As a result, he is unable to perform well, and their future is obliterated. This is due to his parents' decision, which is imposed on him regardless of his interest, because his parents compare him to other fortunate boys in this field and do not understand that it is not mandatory that theirboy also has those facilities. Only they try toimitate others and are unconcerned that theirson is in a stressful situation.

"Imitation is not inspiration, and inspiration only can give birth to a work of art. The least of man's original emanation is better than the best of borrowed thought."

— Albert Pinkham Ryder

It's recondite ourselves, we have to go through a slew of struggles to realise who we are, and very few people attempt to do so. Observing someone else's life from the outside can help us understand our own.

Everyone in this world is unique; it's not a good idea to constantly compare ourselves to others. We try to imitate those whose personalities inspire us, whether consciously or unconsciously. We do not focus on exploring ourselves and destroying our innately obnubilated faculties in this struggle.

When we choose to imitate someone else instead of being ourselves, we are telling God that he made a mistake in creating us the way he did. God adored you and made you unique from everyone else. Nobody will ever be as good as you. Accept yourself for who you are.

Every individual possesses a plethora of strengths and weaknesses. The main goal is to find them. When you try to be someone else, you ignore the forces that exist within yourself. The person you are attempting to imitate is not better than you, but they are unique, which is fine.

Everyone's experience differs from that of others. Imitating other people is pointless because you will never be able to completely replicate their experiences because they are unique to them. You would never be able to be me, and I would never be ableto be you. We are so dissimilar in so many ways, and it is a pulchritudinous fact.

We should seek inspiration from those around us, from all significant people who live on this planet, but resist the temptation to imitate them. There is a distinction to be made between imitating someone and being inspired by someone, and we should be aware of it. Inspiration has the puissance to effect change not just for individuals, but additionally for societies. Technological advancements, remedies for diseases, and solutions to environmental quandaries first emerge as promising conceptions. It is arduous to overstate the paramountcy of deducing for what purport, how, and for whom ingenious conceptions to societal quandaries fire the soul and inspire the conception actualization process.

Rather than attempting to imitate someone, we should seek to discover ourselves, comprehend our true nature, and strive to be ourselves. Let us look for the realus. Allow us to express our true selves; our true individuality is not the one that societyor people want us to be. Let us just be ourselves.

www.ingramcontent.com/pod-product-compliance
Ingram Content Group UK Ltd.
Pitfield, Milton Keynes, MK11 3LW, UK
UKHW022006190726
13853UKWH00004B/1773

9 798885 308120